Greetings from
FLORIDA

FLORIDA

Greetings from
FLORIDA

Greetings from
FLORIDA

Greetings from
FLORIDA

Greetings from
FLORIDA

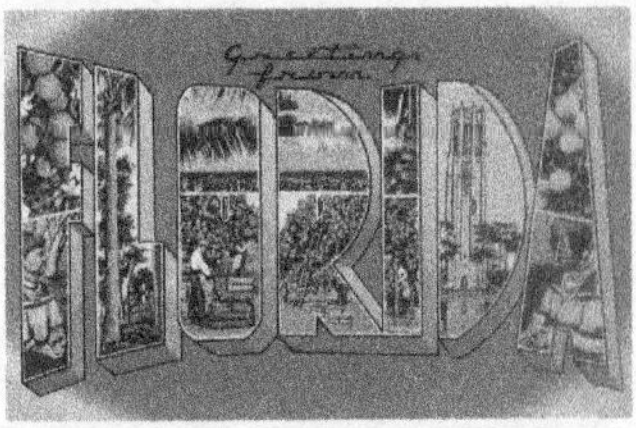
Greetings from
FLORIDA

Greetings from
FLORIDA

Greetings from
FLORIDA

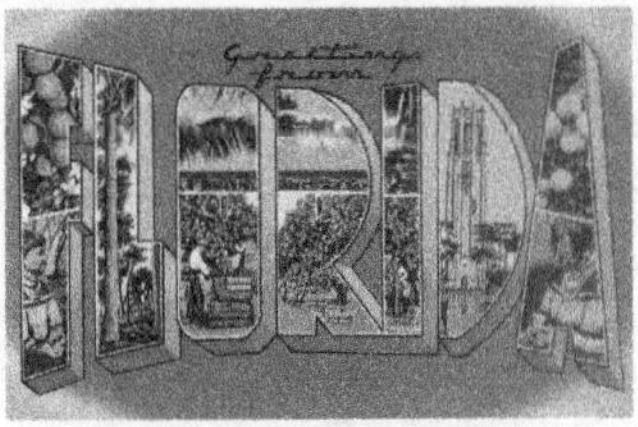
Greetings from
FLORIDA

Greetings from
FLORIDA

Greetings from
FLORIDA

FLORIDA

Greetings from
FLORIDA

Greetings from
FLORIDA

Greetings from
FLORIDA

Greetings from
FLORIDA

Greetings from
FLORIDA

Greetings from
FLORIDA

Greetings from
FLORIDA

Greetings from
FLORIDA

Greetings from
FLORIDA

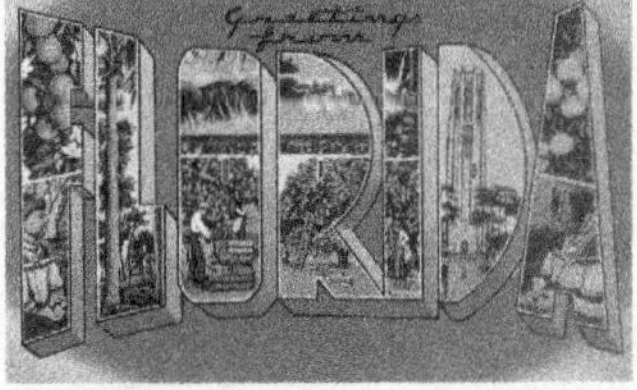
Greetings from
FLORIDA

FLORIDA

Greetings from
FLORIDA

Greetings from
FLORIDA

Greetings from
FLORIDA

FLORIDA

Greetings from
FLORIDA

Greetings from
FLORIDA

Greetings from
FLORIDA

Greetings from
FLORIDA

Greetings from
FLORIDA

Greetings from
FLORIDA

Greetings from
FLORIDA

Greetings from
FLORIDA

Greetings from
FLORIDA

Greetings from
FLORIDA

Greetings from
FLORIDA

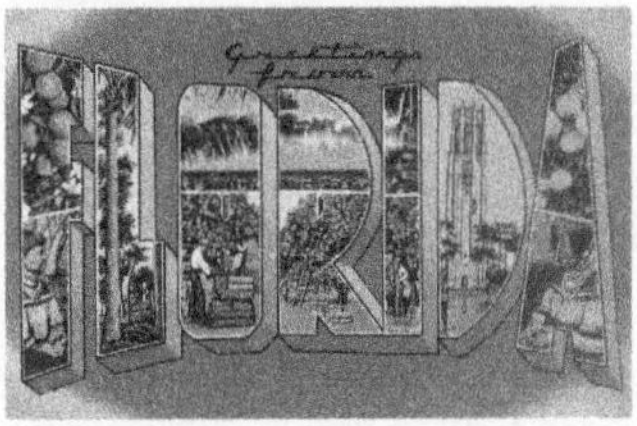
FLORIDA

Greetings from
FLORIDA

Greetings from
FLORIDA

Greetings from
FLORIDA

Greetings from
FLORIDA

Greetings from
FLORIDA

FLORIDA

Greetings from
FLORIDA

Greetings from
FLORIDA

Greetings from
FLORIDA

FLORIDA

Greetings from
FLORIDA

FLORIDA

Greetings from
FLORIDA

Greetings from
FLORIDA

Greetings from
FLORIDA

Greetings from
FLORIDA

Greetings from
FLORIDA

Greetings from
FLORIDA

Greetings from
FLORIDA

Greetings from
FLORIDA

FLORIDA

Greetings from
FLORIDA

Greetings from
FLORIDA

Greetings from
FLORIDA

Greetings from
FLORIDA

Greetings from
FLORIDA

FLORIDA

Greetings
from
FLORIDA

Greetings from
FLORIDA

FLORIDA

Greetings from
FLORIDA

Greetings from
FLORIDA

FLORIDA

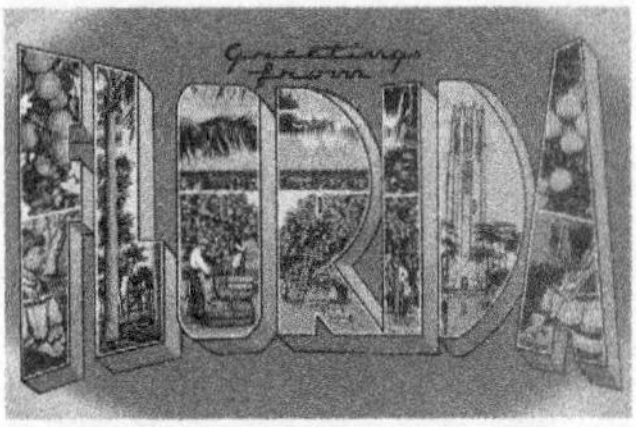
Greetings from
FLORIDA

Greetings from
FLORIDA

Printed in the USA
CPSIA information can be obtained
at www.ICGtesting.com
CBHW020833260624
10675CB00006B/749

9 798385 409648